Praise For A Labor Of Love

"I found the book extremely helpful, friendly, respectful, and full of good ideas. Thanks so much for doing it."
— Laurie P., via e-mail

"Thank you for being there. I gave a eulogy at my grand-mother's funeral. It was amazing...everyone was so moved. I could never have done it without your guidance and kind words. — Robyn A., via e-mail

"I delivered a eulogy at my friend's funeral and it went well. Your book played a major part in my success...As you mentioned, writing does help the grieving process. Even if I hadn't been asked to deliver it, I would have written the eulogy for two people—my friend's wife and myself."
— Steve P., via e-mail

"Don't know what I would have done without your eulogy book. Judging from the comments passed along to me and my wife after the funeral service, I did a great job."
— Joe N., via e-mail

"I wrote eulogies for two people who meant a great deal to me: my sister and a long-time friend. In the process I realized that both had been my mentors. What a gift!"
— Carol N., Brooklyn Park, MN.

"Thanks so much for making the Eulogy Book available over the Internet. This was my first time preparing and delivering a eulogy. The book was a great aid in organizing my thoughts and putting them down on paper."
— Michael B., via e-mail

A Labor of Love

How To Write A Eulogy
by
Garry Schaeffer

Second Edition

GMS PUBLISHING
San Diego, California

To order additional copies, contact:
GMS Publishing
10250 Caminito Cuervo • Suite 23
San Diego, CA 92108
(800) 479-7487 • Fax: (619) 584-1573
e-mail: gms4lafs@adnc.com

ISBN: 0-9645780-1-8

Contents

This book is dedicated to the memory of
Ron Stuart Heimer
1952-1994

Loved by everyone who knew him.

PREFACE

In February of 1993, my wonderful grandfather passed away. I wanted to write a eulogy. I had never written one, so I looked for how-to books in the local library and book stores. Nothing was available. I had an advantage, however, that most people do not have. I was a professional writer.

I sat down, trusted my creative ability, and was eventually pleased with what I wrote; so were my parents, my grandmother, and many friends and relatives who attended the service. I'm sure my grandfather would have been very proud and honored.

In the next 18 months, I wrote two more eulogies; one for my grandmother and one for my best friend who I had known for close to 25 years.

I became convinced that eulogies not only enhance memorial services, making them more personal and meaningful, they also play a valuable part in the healing process. At a time when memories are so important, writing a eulogy brings them to the surface so they can be relived and grieved about. A slow, but certain transformation begins when you preserve those memories on paper and share them with people. Then a eulogy becomes your gift to yourself and others.

I wanted to create a resource that would help people write eulogies and discover the power of writing in the healing process. Writing a eulogy can be a positive experience at a time when nothing seems positive.

I hope this book works for you.

INTRODUCTION

Writing and delivering a eulogy is a noble gesture that is worthy of thought and effort. This is an opportunity to make a contribution to a memorial service—a contribution that your friends and family will remember for a long time. You will not regret the effort that it takes.

You Can Do It.

This is a trying time for you. You may find it difficult to concentrate. Be assured, however, that you can write a eulogy and deliver it. Just follow the steps you will be given and in an hour or so you will have completed a first draft.

For now, keep a positive attitude. Realize that everyone who will attend the memorial service will be supporting you 100 percent. Don't worry about delivering a perfect speech. No one expects you to have the delivery of a great orator or the stage presence of an actor. Just be you; that is enough.

How To Use This Book

If you have very little time—or are not confident about your writing ability—you can go immediately to the Questions section on page 13 and then to the Helpful Phrases on page 21. These will enable you to put something together very quickly.

If you can take some time to write the eulogy—and perhaps be a bit more creative—read and work through the book from start to finish. You will find the sample eulogies, especially those of famous people, to be interesting reading and possibly helpful when you write.

What A Eulogy Should Accomplish

Some people think a eulogy should be an objective summation of a loved one's life. Some people think it should speak for everyone who is present at the funeral. Both of these assumptions are unrealistic.

A eulogy is much more simple. It should convey the feelings and experiences of the person giving the eulogy. The most touching and meaningful eulogies are written from a subjective point of view—and from the heart. So don't feel compelled to write the person's life story. Instead, tell your story.

Clearly, the burden of the eulogy does not have to be yours completely. If you have the time, ask friends or relatives for their recollections and stories. In a eulogy, it is perfectly acceptable to say, "I was talking to Uncle Lenny about Ron; he reminded me of the time Ron came to our Thanksgiving dinner with half of his face clean-shaven and the other half bearded. It was Ron's funny way of showing that he had mixed feelings about shaving off his beard."

Honesty is very important. In most cases, there will be a lot of positive things to say about your loved one. Once in a while, there is someone with more negative traits than positive qualities. If that is the case, remember, you don't have to say everything. Just be honest about the positive qualities and everyone will appreciate the eulogy.

Remember, you do not have to write a perfect eulogy. Whatever you write will be appreciated by the people at the funeral. If you are inclined to be a perfectionist, lower your expectations and just do what you can given the short time-frame and your emotional state.

9

GETTING STARTED

When you contemplate writing a eulogy, it is important to overcome the inertia that fear and doubts can create. Many questions come to mind: "What will I say?" "How will I say it?" "Can I actually write a eulogy?" "Do I have enough time?" "Will I do a good job?" "How do I get started?"

These and many more questions will be answered in this book. Writing a eulogy is easier than you may think. Please put your fears aside and be assured that you can do it. The trick is to break it down into small, manageable tasks, which are:

- **Outline the eulogy**.
  It is much easier to write after you've gathered your thoughts.
- **Write the first draft**.
  This can be done more quickly than you might imagine.
- **Put the eulogy aside for a while**.
  Taking a break will give you more objectivity.
- **Come back later to edit and polish it**.
  Making changes will be easier when you are fresh.

Keep in mind that no important document is written in one sitting. Instead, it is pieced together like a puzzle. (A lack of time may force you to write a eulogy in one sitting, which can be done.) Let's get started.

GATHERING YOUR THOUGHTS

Why should you create an outline? Some people can sit down and write brilliantly off the top of their heads; and some people can speak extemporaneously and still be eloquent. Most of us, however, should use outlines to write and notes to speak.

I recommend you outline the eulogy for several reasons:

- It will keep you focused.
- It keep the eulogy organized.
- An outline will prevent the writing process from becoming a frustrating experience.
- It will help you explore your subject thoroughly, so you won't forget important details.
- An outline will help you break down the writing into small, manageable pieces.

An outline can be as detailed as you wish. In fact, the more details, the faster you will write. The writing will flow from one subject to the next because you will see precisely where you are going with your ideas.

HOW TO OUTLINE BY CLUSTERING

The best way to outline is by clustering. (also known as "mind-mapping") As you will see, clustering is done in a circle, rather than vertically down a page.

Clustering stimulates creative thinking because you do not have to explore one topic at a time. Instead, you are free to jump from one idea to the next, no matter how unrelated your thoughts may be. There is no logical order in clustering; the order is created later.

Clustering loosens your thinking and puts you in an exploratory frame of mind. With clustering, you will generate new ideas quickly and easily. Here is how it works:

Write the name of the person in the middle of a large piece of paper. Circle the name. Think of an area to explore. Draw a spoke out from the circle and write a key word or phrase that relates to that topic; for example, "sense of humor." Keep doing this as ideas come to mind. To add details to a topic, draw a line out from it and add more key words or phrases—just enough to jog your memory. Move around the circle with new ideas and extend out from existing topics at random, as the following cluster illustrates:

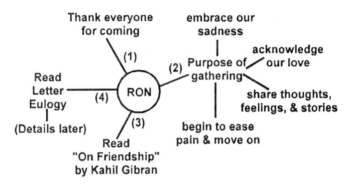

An expanded version of this cluster can be found on page 64 Two more cluster outlines—and the eulogies to which they relate—appear on pages 61 and 67.

After you have thought of many areas to write about (see the next page for help), go back over the cluster and number the main ideas in the order in which they should be addressed. This order can change later. For now, it creates more structure for your writing. Keep in mind that you may decide later to eliminate some topics, which is fine.

Clustering is also helpful while you are writing. If you suddenly find yourself at a loss for ideas, take a fresh piece of paper and begin clustering an outline around the topic on which you are stuck. New ideas will surface quickly. Stop to do this as many times as necessary to evoke all the memories about which you want to write.

Create Your Outline

If you want, take the time now to create an outline, or wait until you have read the next section or the entire book.

WHAT TO WRITE ABOUT

There are so many aspects of your loved one to talk about; however, you may still go blank because you are not thinking clearly at this time. To stimulate your thoughts and help you focus on important ideas, you might find it helpful to answer some—not all—of the following questions. As you read these questions, jot down notes or start a cluster outline. When possible, think of poignant or humorous stories that illustrate the qualities that you will write about.

- How long did you know your loved one?
- How did you meet him/her? (if this is note-worthy)
- How did he/she show his/her love for you and others?
- Was this person active in the community? How?
- Was he/she active in professional associations?
- What were some of your loved one's most endearing qualities? (e.g., kindness, compassion, sensitivity, thoughtfulness, generosity, sense of humor, liveliness?)
- How would you describe his/her relationship(s) with spouse, children, relatives, and close friends?

- What kind of mother, father, son, daughter, friend, was this person?
- If you had to think of one quality that he or she will be remembered for, what would it be? Why?
- Why were you inspired to write this eulogy?
- What do you want everyone to know and/or remember about this person?
- What are some of your fond memories and how have those events affected your life?

Do you find these questions thought-provoking? Don't forget to put these ideas into a clustered outline. Here are more questions to stimulate your creativity:

- What made your loved one happy?
- What did he/she do to have fun?
- What made him/her sad?
- How would he/she want to be remembered?
- What attracted this person's friends to him/her?
- What kept you together all these years?

Think of a role that this person played in your life. (e.g., mother, father, son, daughter, friend, boss; the person who introduced you to fishing, cooking, waterskiing, dancing, surfing, painting, etc.) Think of a story that illustrates the unique way that he/she played this role.

- Is there a philosophy that this person lived by? What is it? Provide a story to illustrate.
- What did you learn about life from him/her?
- What will you remember most about this person? Why? Can you tell a story that illustrates this?

- What did this person give to the world or the people around him or her.
- What were some of this person's favorite things? And what do these things say about him/her?
- Are there any accomplishments of which this person was very proud?
- What was a major accomplishment for this person?
- What accomplishment are you most proud of?
- Can you think of a colorful story that succinctly portrays or sums up this person's personality?

WRITING THE FIRST DRAFT

Now that you have outlined the eulogy—and numbered the ideas in your cluster—you are ready to write; well, almost. Before you begin, read the following tips. They will help you start the creative flow:

- **Don't expect perfection in the first draft**. It is not easy to put your thoughts on paper. This is especially true now, when you are not in top form emotionally. Certainly your thinking is less clear than normal. If the words do not come to you easily now, please do not panic, freeze, or give up. Instead, take consolation in knowing that editing is an important step in the writing process. You will have an opportunity later to improve your first draft.

- **Don't be afraid of the unknown**. Start writing without the need to know exactly what you will say or where the writing will take you. Follow your outline and let the words pour out.

- **Writing requires a warm-up period**. Writing is very much like playing a sport; you have to warm up.

Don't expect to sit down and immediately write a stream of well-organized thoughts. Be content with starting slowly. One way to get your creative juices flowing is to write a letter to your loved one. After you have warmed up, answer some of the questions that were provided above. Keep the writing going and work your way into the outline that you have created.

If you like the idea of writing a letter, consider using the letter-writing technique for the eulogy itself. See "The Letter Eulogy" on page 21.

• **Write nonjudgmentally**. This tip is also very important. Write as quickly as possible and make absolutely no judgments about what you have written. Don't stop to search for the perfect word or to correct spelling errors; do that later. Instead, tap into a stream of thoughts and let them flow uninterrupted.

THE OPENING OF A EULOGY

There are many ways to introduce a eulogy; some are described below. It is important to realize that the opening of any written piece can be the most difficult part to write. An opening may not occur to you right away. That is okay. If an opening sentence or concept is not forthcoming, skip it. Instead, state the topic plainly (e.g., "This is a eulogy about Ron.") and start writing. You can come back later to create a better opening sentence. Ideally, an opening sentence should draw in your audience; it should be compelling. Perhaps one of the following techniques will make sense for the opening of the eulogy you will write:

Quotes. A moving, spiritual, or amusing quote can be effective. You can quote your loved one or someone famous. You can use a quote from the Bible or other inspirational book. You may find a useful quote in Bartlett's Quotations or a book of poems. For example, a eulogy could begin with, "The great writer, W. Somerset Maugham, once wrote, 'The great tragedy of life is not that men perish, but that they cease to love.' Sarah never ceased to love. Everyone called her 'Sweet Sarah' because she was one of the most loving people we have ever known...."

Anecdotes. Anecdotes, like quotes, should reveal a quality that your loved one possessed. Humor is acceptable, even encouraged, in many cultures, but it must be relevant and in good taste. Humor is valuable because people need to remember the joy and gain some momentary relief from the sadness.

Here is an example of a humorous anecdote: "I take some consolation in the good feelings that my memories provide. I remember staying overnight at my grandparent's house when I was five years old. The three of us slept in one big bed. I laughed so hard in the morning when my grandfather told me, 'Boy, are you a restless sleeper! I woke up in the middle of the night and your foot was in my mouth, the other foot was in my ear!'"

Philosophical Inspiration. If it is your style, begin with a philosophical statement. For example, "I can't help being struck by an irony. Allan was a modest man. He disliked being the center of attention. As such, he would have felt self-conscious about this service and everyone's attention being focused on him. Instead, he would have wanted us to change our focus from him to us. He would have wanted us to dwell not on who we have lost, but on who we still have. He would have wanted us to use this time to look within and gain a new appreciation of everyone in our lives. He would have wanted us to find new ways to make our time together more precious."

Problems. Posing a problem and its solution can be very dramatic. This type of opening might sound like this: "In 1935, a 10-year old boy found out what it means to be a man. His father died suddenly. His mother suffered from polio and could not work. His younger brother and sister were barely old enough to tie their shoes. So this 10-year old man shouldered the responsibility of supporting his family. By the age of 15, he ran a newspaper delivery service with ten employees. At 35 he owned three major newspapers, four radio stations, and a TV station. His sense of responsibility for his family never turned to greed. In fact, giving became his passion. Few individuals are capable of the type of philanthropy that changes people's lives. Today there are hospitals, museums, performing arts centers, and university libraries that bear this man's name. That 10-year old boy was my older brother, one of the most remarkable men of his time."

Questions. Begin by asking a thought-provoking question; and be sure to give the answer. For example: "I once asked Mike, 'What is most important to you in life? Success? Learning a lot? Having fun?' He said, 'Striking a balance between enjoying the moment and providing for the future. After all, it's the highlights that we remember in life, but great moments are only possible if you are responsible and create the means for having them.' Those were two major themes in Mike's life: having fun and being responsible."

Juxtaposition. You can create an interesting opening by contrasting two seemingly unrelated facts. "Joe drove a new BMW, owned a $450,000 house, had a million dollar stock portfolio, and bragged about never having finished high school. How did he do it? Vision, dedication, and a healthy respect for people."

Sensationalism. Shock people and they will listen, but don't over-do it. For example, "Linda knew there was a killer on the loose. She had dedicated her entire professional career to fighting it, never knowing that it was lurking in every shadow that she cast. It is ironic and sad that, in the prime of her life, Linda would become one of its victims. Dr. Linda Smith was a highly-respected oncologist. The monster, of course, is cancer."

Statistics. Unless they open your listeners' eyes, statistics can be boring. Use them cautiously. Combine statistics with sensationalism, however, and you can create a powerful opening. For example, "By the year 2000, one out of two people will have known someone who has died of AIDS. This is no longer someone else's disease."

THE MIDDLE OF A EULOGY

The body of a eulogy follows the opening. Start with the first topic in your outline and write as much as you can. Write with an informal, conversational tone, as if you were speaking. When you have either concluded the first topic or run out of steam, move on to the next topic in your outline. The more topics you have outlined, the easier the writing will. Simply go from one topic to the next, addressing them the best you can. If they are incomplete, don't worry about it now.

Your discussion of a topic can be as short as a paragraph or as long as several pages. You should strive, however, to make the length of a discussion proportionate to the importance of the topic.

If you are not comfortable as a writer, keep in mind that each paragraph should relate to the topic being discussed. (Cover one idea at a time, then move on.) At the same time, each sentence in a paragraph should relate to the ideas only in that paragraph. If you find writing difficult, try writing a List Eulogy—discussed below—or use the helpful phrases that are provided later.

As you write, new ideas will pop up. Remember that thoughts can be as fleeting as shooting stars—brilliant yet short-lived—so seize them by either taking notes or writing about the idea immediately. You can always re-arrange paragraphs later, especially if you work on a computer.

The List Eulogy

To make writing a eulogy very easy, you can use a format that I call the "list eulogy." A list eulogy is little more than a list with examples and stories provided for each item on the list. The list eulogy is easy because you do not have to write in a narrative style.

The list eulogy should be introduced with a compelling opening. Next, preface the list with an introductory statement, such as, "Ron was truly one in a billion. I can think of at least eight ways that he made the world a better place..."

After the set-up, present your list, one item at a time. For example, you might say, "First, he had the most charming, off-beat sense of humor. I remember the time he..." (Then provide a story that illustrates the point.) He also lived life to the fullest..." (Provide another example.) Resist the temptation to merely list reasons. It is the stories that make a eulogy come to life.

You can see how your list and the explanations of each point would form the body of the eulogy. A list eulogy is easier for some people. You should consider this format if you find it difficult to capture your thoughts on paper.

The Letter Eulogy

If writing a letter is relatively easy for you, pretend you are writing a letter to your loved one, a friend, or a relative. In the letter, talk about everything in your outline. Let your thoughts flow freely as you would when writing a personal letter. Don't worry about transitions between sections; an informal tone is acceptable. When you are finished writing the letter, put it aside and come back to edit and polish it later. (See page 65 for an example of a letter eulogy.)

HELPFUL PHRASES

The following phrases may help you express the way you feel. You can use them verbatim, modify them, or just become inspired by them. To use them as the basis of a eulogy, pick a phrase and then fill in some details. For example, you might choose, "He was a kind, loving husband," but don't stop there, include a story or an example that shows how he was a kind, loving husband. Keep doing this with many phrases until you are done. These phrases and the questions in the section, What To Write About (page 13), will help you write a first draft.

For the phrases that follow, keep in mind: 1) The words in parentheses are options. Choose one or insert your own. 2) Where it says, (Name), insert either the person's name or the appropriate pronoun, "he" or "she." 3) Where you see an ellipsis (. . .), finish the sentence.

- It is difficult to put my feelings into words, but I will try to tell you what (Name) meant to me.

- (Name) was a loving mother (father, son, daughter, etc.)
- (Name) was a kind, loving wife (husband, etc.) who...
- (Name) had a beauty of character that endeared her to all who crossed her path.
- (Name) will be missed. I will always remember his/her laugh (or choose a noun from below).
- <u>Nouns</u>: smile, sense of humor, grace, charm, elegance, generosity, radiance, cheerfulness, beautiful eyes, innocence, playfulness, sincerity, kind words, etc.
- (Name) gave so much to his family (community, temple, church, profession, etc.)
- His/her parting creates a void that will never be filled.
- (Name) will long be remembered as someone who...
- I have fond memories of (Name) and will cherish them for ever. (This is a good ending.)
- There is pain and sorrow to bear, but, in time, we will be comforted by the warmth of our memories.
- I consider myself fortunate to possess a wealth of wonderful memories. (This is a good ending.)
- In the end, the true measure of a person is not the wealth left behind, but the richness of the memories he or she gave to others.
- (Name) has enriched my life immeasurably. (This is a good way to end a eulogy.)
- The true measure of a person, in the final analysis, is the lasting impression that he/she has made on people.
- In this time of mourning, I know my strength will come, in part, from my appreciation of the wonderful memories that (Name) has given me.
- (Name)'s strength of character showed us that . . . (describe a lesson that was learned).

22

- I like to think that (Name) is with us in spirit, and always will be.
- It is comforting to know that (Name) has gone to a better place.
- (Name) would want us to be strong and to carry on by . . . (e.g., keeping his name alive by. . .; remembering the good times; comforting each other; etc.)
- The wonderful turn-out today is a (loving) testimony to the contribution that (Name) made to the lives of his/her family and friends.
- If I had to choose one word to describe (Name), it would be...
- I will always be grateful for (Name)'s (love, friendship, companionship, guidance, etc.)
- He/she was a (choose several nouns from below), all in one.
  Nouns: husband, wife, best friend, confidant, lover, cheerleader, mentor, counselor, son, daughter, mother, father, coach, business associate, business partner, teacher, inspiration, motivator, role model, etc.
- Some of the greatest moments of my life were shared with (Name). In fact, he/she helped make them great moments. (This phrase should be followed by a story or an example.)
- When we look back, it is the great moments and the great people that we cherish and remember in life. (Name) was one of those great people.
- We have all lost a true friend.
- I have never known a more kind and gentle (or fill in other adjectives from below) man/woman.
  Adjectives: Considerate, thoughtful, loving, fun,

ambitious, entertaining, funny, compassionate, lively, generous, selfless, honest, caring, sincere, supportive, down-to-earth, passionate, enthusiastic, energetic, etc.

- (Name) and I had a special relationship (friendship, marriage, etc.); he/she was like a father (mother, a second father, a second mother, brother, sister, son, or daughter) to me.
- (Name) was always willing to ... (lend a hand, offer advice, listen, help someone in need, go the extra mile, give without expecting something in return, stand up for what he/she believed was right, etc.)
- Life was all-too-short for (Name).
- His/her life was full of love (laughter, family, friends)
- (Name) loved a challenge and met each one straight on (or with resolve, with determination, with a drive to win, with courage, courageously, gallantly, etc.)
- I feel blessed to have known (Name).
- It was a pleasure and a privilege to have known (Name)
- I know (Name) would want all of you to know that he loved you dearly.
- Before (Name) died, he/she told me . . .
- I feel a sense of closure with (Name) because...
- I don't feel a sense of closure with (Name) because...
- (Name) always said (or always believed) that . . .
- She/he helped me understand the meaning of ..... (love, friendship, fun, devotion, commitment, success, generosity, thoughtfulness, life, service, humility, etc.)
- I can thank (Name) for . . .
- If it weren't for (Name), I wouldn't . . .
- (Name) will be missed. Very much. And forever.

ENDING A EULOGY

The ending should be a brief paragraph that wraps up everything into a neat package. A good conclusion gives the listener a feeling of closure. A conclusion is not the place to throw in miscellaneous thoughts that should have been included earlier; nor is it the place to start a new train of thought. Instead, a good conclusion accomplishes at least one of the following:

- It summarizes how your loved one impacted your life.
- It restates an important point briefly.
- It raises an important question and answers it; e.g., what does the future hold?
- It uses a quote to support an important theme in the eulogy.
- It emphasizes a need for a change in attitude or behavior.

Clichéd endings should be avoided. For example, never begin an ending with, "In conclusion," "To summarize," or "Last, but not least..." Avoid gushing with exaggerations. Your love and devotion will have shone through in the body of the eulogy, so don't over-do it at the end.

The Ideal Length

The ideal length for a eulogy is long enough to say everything that is important to you, but short enough to hold everyone's attention. Five to eight minutes is a good goal. This will translate into three to seven double-spaced, type-written pages, depending on how fast you speak.

Put It Aside Now

The next step is to stop working on the eulogy. Put it aside and think about other things. Depending on your time-frame, this could be a couple of hours—or a couple of days. This rest will enable you to come back to your work with more objectivity. An objective writer is better able to don the critic's hat and calmly trim away the excess, rewrite the awkward, and add important ingredients.

EDITING AND POLISHING

The next step is to fix what you have written. The editing process is necessary because few people can write a "perfect" first draft. It pays to take the time to edit and polish your eulogy. Please resist the temptation to skip this phase. To make your words sound like music—harmonious and pleasing to the ear—follow the advice below as you edit:

Be Brief. If your first draft is rather long, look for what you can cut, not what you can add. Be sure you have said everything concisely. Anecdotes, humorous asides, and philosophical thoughts are informative and entertaining in moderation—and when they are brief and relevant.

To write concisely, sharpen your focus. For each point that you make about your loved one, paint a picture with specific examples and then move on to the next point. Outlining the eulogy before you write will help you do this.

Write for your listeners. Writing about ideas is fine for some subjects, but for a eulogy, write about people— you, your loved one, relatives, and friends. People may not be receptive to your philosophies, but they will appreciate stories that show the human, lovable side of your loved one.

Write with confidence. Make self-assured statements. Avoid sounding indirect or tentative. For example, instead of saying, "Some of you may have, on occasion, experienced

Ron's sense of humor;" you should say, "Ron had a quick wit and a refreshing sense of the absurd."

Write as if you were speaking. Earlier, you were told to write conversationally—as if you were writing a letter to a friend. The best style is fluid, relaxed, and not stuffy. This book is an example of a conversational writing style.

Vary the lengths of sentences. Hold your listeners' attention and sound conversational by varying the lengths of your sentences. This sentence has five words. Five-word sentences are fine. Too many often become dull. You can see for yourself. This is beginning to drone. A better tack is to vary the lengths of your sentences, and, by doing so, create waves of sound that keep the listener tuned in. Use short sentences for emphasis. Long sentences convey complex thoughts. Used in moderation, both lengths are effective.

Use the ends of sentences for emphasis. The end of a sentence has more emphasis than the beginning or middle. Place the phrase or word that you wish to emphasize at the end of a sentence. For example, "As employers go, Ron was the best. He was fun to work with, full of creative ideas, and generous with his praise, especially for himself."

Alternate the use of the person's name with the pronoun. A eulogy sounds best when the person's name is mentioned in every other sentence—more or less—and the pronoun "he" or "she" used the rest of the time.

TIPS FOR DELIVERING A EULOGY

This may be the most difficult speech you will ever give, but it will be the most rewarding. It is important to realize that people in the audience will not judge you. They will be very supportive. No matter what happens, it will be okay. If you break down in the middle of the speech, everyone will understand. Take a moment to compose yourself, then continue. There is no reason to be embarrassed. Remember, giving a eulogy is a noble gesture that people will appreciate and admire.

If you can, make the eulogy easy to read. On a computer, print out the eulogy in a large type size. If you are using a typewriter, put extra carriage returns between the lines. If you are writing it by hand, print the final version in large letters and give the words room to breath by writing on every second or third line.

Before the memorial service, consider getting a small cup of water. Keep it with you during the service. When you go to the podium to deliver the eulogy, take the water with you in case you need it. Sipping water before you start—and during the speech, if needed—will help relax you.

If you are nervous before delivering the eulogy, breath deeply and tell yourself that everything will be fine. It really will be. Look around at your relatives and friends and realize that they are with you 100 percent. It is acceptable to read the eulogy without making eye contact with the audience, if that would be easier for you. Take your time. Do the best you can. No one expects you to have the delivery of a great orator or the stage presence of an actor. Just be you.

SAMPLE EULOGIES

It helps to learn by example. The following eulogies are interesting to read. They are also inspiring and moving.

At first glance, some of the language may sound grandiose, over-dramatic, or too poetic. You might consider several things: 1) some of these eulogies were written for great people whose tragic deaths affected entire nations and, in some cases, the course of a country's history; 2) the eulogies were often written by statesmen and others who possessed impressive writing and oratory skills; and 3) every loss of a human being is tragic and devastating to those who knew and loved him or her, so what seems grandiose to outsiders may sound just right to loved ones.

Read the following eulogies and, if you dare, flourish the one that you write with majestic phrases; dare to reach for the stars by waxing poetic. You are, after all, conveying to your audience the importance and effect that your loved one had on you (and perhaps on many others). No one can minimize, diminish, or question the depth or significance of your love. Write whatever you want with whatever language is appropriate to express your feelings, as long as you are honest.

EULOGY FOR MOHANDAS GANDHI
by Jawaharlal Nehru
India's Former Prime Minister
February 2, 1948

A glory has departed and the sun that warmed and brightened our lives has set, and we shiver in the cold and dark. Yet he would not have us feel this way. After all, glory that we saw for all these years, that man with the divine fire, changed us also—and such as we are, we have been molded by him during these years; and out of that divine fire many of us also took a small spark which strengthened and made us work to some extent on the lines that he fashioned. And so if we praise him, our words seem rather small, and if we praise him, to some extent we also praise ourselves. Great men and eminent men have monuments in bronze and marble

30

set up for them, but this man of divine fire managed in his lifetime to become enshrined in millions and millions of hearts so that all of us became somewhat of the stuff that he was made of, though to an infinitely lesser degree. He spread out in this way all over India, not in palaces only, or in select places or in assemblies, but in every hamlet and hut of the lowly and those who suffer. He lives in the hearts of millions and he will live for immemorial ages.

What, then, can we say about him except to feel humble on this occasion? To praise him we are not worthy—to praise him whom we could not follow adequately and sufficiently. It is almost doing him an injustice just to pass him by with words when he demanded work and labor and sacrifice from us; in a large measure he made this country, during the last thirty years or more, attain to heights of sacrifice which in that particular domain have never been equaled elsewhere. He succeeded in that. Yet ultimately things happened which no doubt made him suffer tremendously, though his tender face never lost its smile and he never spoke a harsh word to anyone. Yet, he must have suffered—suffered for the failing of this generation whom he had trained, suffered because we went away from the path that he had shown us. And ultimately the hand of a child of his—for he, after all, is as much a child of his as any other Indian—the hand of a child of his struck him down.

Long ages afterwards history will judge of this period that we have passed through. It will judge of the successes and the failures—we are too near it to be proper judges and to understand what has happened and what has not happened. All we know is that there was a glory and that it is no more; all we know is that for a moment there is darkness, not so dark certainly, because when we look into our hearts we still find the living flame which he lighted there. And if those living flames exist, there will not be darkness in this land, and we shall be able, with our effort, remembering him and following his path, to illumine this land again, small as we are, but still with the fire that he instilled into us.

He was perhaps the greatest symbol of the India of the past, and may I say, of the India of the future, that we could have had. We stand on this perilous edge of the present, between that past and the future to be, and we face all manner of perils. And the greatest peril is sometimes the lack of faith which comes to us, the sense of frustration that comes to us, the sinking of the heart and of the spirit that comes to us when we see ideals go overboard, when we see the great things that we talked about somehow pass into empty words, and life taking a different course. Yet, I do believe that perhaps this period will pass soon enough.

He has gone, and all over India there is a feeling of having been left desolate and forlorn. All of us sense that feeling, and I do not know how we shall be able to get rid of it. And yet together with that feeling there is also a feeling of proud thankfulness that it has been given to us of this generation to be associated with this mighty person. In ages to come, centuries and maybe millennia after us, people will think of this generation when this man of God trod on earth, and will think of us who, however small, could also follow his path and tread the holy ground where his feet had been. Let us be worthy of him.

EULOGY FOR JOHN F. KENNEDY
Delivered in the rotunda of the
U.S. Capital by Mike Mansfield
Senate Majority Leader
November 24, 1963

There was a sound of laughter; in a moment, it was no more. And so she took a ring from her finger and placed it in his hands.

There was a wit in a man neither young nor old, but a wit full of an old man's wisdom and of a child's wisdom, and then, in a moment it was no more. And so she took a ring from her finger and placed it in his hands.

There was a man marked with scars of his love of country, a body active with the surge of a life far, far from spent and, in a moment, it was no more. And so she took a ring from her finger and placed it in his hands.

There was a father with a little boy, a little girl and a joy of each in the other. In a moment it was no more, and so she took a ring from her finger and placed it in his hands.

There was a husband who asked much and gave much, and out of the giving and the asking wove with a woman what could not be broken in life, and in a moment it was no more. And so she took a ring from her finger and placed it in his hands, and kissed him and closed the lid of a coffin.

A piece of each of us died at that moment. Yet, in death he gave of himself to us. He gave us of a good heart from which the laughter came. He gave us of a profound wit, from which a great leadership emerged. He gave us of a kindness and a strength fused into a human courage to seek peace without fear.

He gave us of his love that we, too, in turn, might give. He gave that we might give of ourselves, that we might give to one another until there would be no room, no room at all, for the bigotry, the hatred, prejudice, and the arrogance which converged in that moment of horror to strike him down.

In leaving us—these gifts, John Fitzgerald Kennedy, President of the United States, leaves with us. Will we take them, Mr. President? Will we have, now, the sense and the responsibility and the courage to take them?

I pray to God that we shall and under God we will.

EULOGY FOR JOHN F. KENNEDY
by Earl Warren
Chief Justice of the United States
November 24, 1963

There are few events in our national life that unite Americans and so touch the hearts of all of us as the passing of a President of the United States.

There is nothing that adds shock to our sadness as the assassination of our leader, chosen as he is to embody the ideals of our people, the faith we have in our institutions and our belief in the fatherhood of God and the brotherhood of man.

Such misfortunes have befallen the Nation on other occasions, but never more shockingly than two days ago.

We are saddened; we are stunned; we are perplexed.

John Fitzgerald Kennedy, a great and good President, the friend of all men of good will, a believer in the dignity and equality of all human beings, a fighter for justice, an apostle of peace, has been snatched from our midst by the bullet of an assassin.

What moved some misguided wretch to do this horrible deed may never be known to us, but we do know that such acts are commonly stimulated by forces of hatred and malevolence, such as today are eating their way into the bloodstream of American life. What a price we pay for this fanaticism.

It has been said that the only thing we learn from history is that we do not learn. But surely we can learn if we have the will to do so. Surely there is a lesson to be learned from this tragic event.

If we really love this country, if we truly love justice and mercy, if we fervently want to make this Nation better for those who are to follow us, we can at least abjure the hatred that consumes people, the false accusations that divide us, and the bitterness that begets violence. Is it too much to hope that the martyrdom of our beloved President might even soften the hearts of those who would themselves recoil from assassination, but who do not shrink from spreading the venom which kindles thoughts of it in others?

Our Nation is bereaved. The whole world is poorer because of his loss. But we can all be better Americans because John Fitzgerald Kennedy has passed our way, because he has been our chosen leader at a time in history when his character, his vision, and his quiet courage have enabled him to chart for us a safe course through the shoals of treacherous seas that encompass the world.

And now that he is relieved of the almost superhuman burdens we imposed on him, may he rest in peace.

EULOGY FOR JOHN F. KENNEDY
by John W. McCormick
Speaker of the House of Representatives
November 24, 1963

...Any citizen of our beloved country who looks back over its history cannot fail to see that we have been blessed with God's favor beyond most other peoples. At each great crisis to our history we have found a leader able to grasp the helm of state and guide the country through the troubles which beset it. In our earliest days, when our strength and wealth were so limited and our problems so great, Washington and Jefferson appeared to lead our people. Two generations later, when our country was torn in two by a fratricidal war, Abraham Lincoln appeared from the mass of the people as a leader able to reunite the Nation.

In more recent times, in the critical days of the depression and the great war forced upon us by Fascist aggression, Franklin Delano Roosevelt—later, Harry S. Truman—appeared on the scene to reorganize the country and lead its revived citizens to victory. Finally, only recently, when the cold war was building up the supreme crisis of a threatened nuclear war capable of destroying everything—and every-body—that our predecessors had so carefully built, and which a liberty-loving world wanted, once again a strong and courageous man appeared ready to lead us.

No country need despair so long as God, in His infinite goodness, continues to provide the Nation with leaders able to guide it through the successive crises which seem to be the inevitable fate of any great nation.

Surely no country ever faced more gigantic problems than ours in the last few years, and surely no country could have obtained a more able leader in a time of such crises. President John Fitzgerald Kennedy possessed all the qualities of greatness. He had deep faith, complete confidence, human sympathy, and broad vision which recognized the true values of freedom, equality, and the brotherhood which have always been the marks of the American political dreams.

He had the bravery and a sense of personal duty which made him willing to face up to the great task of being President in these trying times. He had the warmth and the sense of humanity which made the burden of the task bearable for himself and for his associates, and which made all kinds of diverse peoples and races eager to be associated with him in his task. He had the tenacity and determination to carry each stage of his great work through to its successful conclusion.

Now that our great leader has been taken from us in a cruel death, we are bound to feel shattered and helpless in the face of our loss. This is but natural, but as the first bitter pangs of our incredulous grief begins to pass we must thank God that we were privileged, however briefly, to have had this great man for our President. For he has now taken his place among the great figures of world history.

While this is an occasion of deep sorrow it should be also one of dedication. We must have the determination to unite and carry on the spirit of John Fitzgerald Kennedy for a strengthened America and a future world of peace.

EULOGY FOR JOHN F. KENNEDY
by Senator Everett McKinley Dirksen
November 25, 1963

The memory of John Fitzgerald Kennedy lingers in this forum of the people. Here we knew his vigorous tread, his flashing smile, his ready wit, his keen mind, his zest for adventure. Here with quiet grief we mourn his departure. Here we shall remember him best as a colleague whose star of public service is indelibly inscribed on the roll of the United States Senate.

And here the eternal question confronts and confounds us. Why must it be? Why must the life of an amiable, friendly, aggressive young man, moved only by high motives, lighted on his way by high hopes, guided by broad plans, impelled by understanding and vision, be brought to an untimely end and with his labor unfinished.

And why, in a free land, untouched by the heel of dictatorship and oppression, where the humblest citizen may freely utter his grievances, must that life be cut short by an evil instrument, moved by malice, frustration, and hate? This is the incredible thing which leaves us bewildered and perplexed.

One moment there is the ecstasy of living when one can hear the treble cries of scampering children over the White House lawn, the pleasure of receiving a Thanksgiving turkey which I presented to him but three days before the evil deed, the pleasure of conversation over many things including his hopes for the future, the exciting fact of sunshine and green grass in late November, the endless stream of saluting crowds, and then the sudden strangling death rattle of dissolution. Who shall say, save that there is a divinity which shapes our ends and marks our days.

As the tumult and grief subside, as the nation resumes and moves forward, and his own generation measures his works and achievements, what shall we say who knew him well—we who knew him best not as Mr. President, but simply as Jack.

We saw him come to the Senate at age 35. We saw him grow. We saw him rise. We saw him elevated to become the Chief Magistrate of this nation. And we saw him as the leader of both branches of this Republic assembled to deliberate over common problems.

In this moment when death has triumphed, when hearts are chastened, when the spirit reels in sheer bewilderment, what do we say, now that the book of life has been closed?

Let me say what we have always said when he was alive, gay, happy, friendly, ambitious and ready to listen.

He had vision that went beyond our own. His determination to effectuate a test-ban treaty is a living example.

He was his own profile in courage. His unrelenting devotion to equality and civil rights attests that fact.

He was devoted to our system of constitutional government. His attitude toward the separation of church and state looms like a shining example.

He had the great virtue of spiritual grace. If at any moment he may have seemed frustrated over a proposition, it was so transitory. If he showed any sign of petulance, it was so fleeting. There were no souring acids in his spirit. If, at any moment, he may have seemed over-eager, it was but the reflection of a zealous crusader and missioner who knew where he was going.

If, at any moment, he seemed to depart from the covenant which he and his party made with the people, it was only because he believed that accelerated events and circumstances did not always heed the clock and the calendar. If his course sometimes seemed at variance with his own party leaders or with the opposition, it was only because a deep conviction dictated his course.

On the tablets of memory, we who knew him well as a friend and colleague, can well inscribe this sentiment:

Senator John Fitzgerald Kennedy, who became the 35th President of the United States—young, vigorous, aggressive and scholarly—one who estimated the needs of his country and the world and sought to fulfill that need— one who was wedded to peace and vigorously sought this greatest of all goals of mankind—one who sensed how catastrophic nuclear conflict could be and sought a realistic course to avert it—one who sensed the danger that lurked in a continuing inequality in our land and sought a rational and durable solution—one to whom the phrase "the national interest" was more than a string of words—one who could disagree without vindictiveness—one who believed that the expansion of the enjoyment of living by all people was an achievable goal—one who believed that each generation must contribute its best to the fulfillment of the American dream.

The *Te Deums* which will be sung this day may be wafted away by the evening breeze which caresses the last resting place of those who served the Republic, but here in this chamber where he served and prepared for higher responsibility, the memory of John Fitzgerald Kennedy will long linger to nourish the faith of all who serve that same great land.

EULOGY FOR DR. MARTIN LUTHER KING, JR.

by Reverend Ralph D. Abernathy,
co-pastor with Dr. King of the
Ebenezer Baptist Church
April 9, 1968

Members of the bereaved family, distinguished citizens of the world, ladies and gentlemen.

To your great delight, I'm cutting about five minutes off of this eulogy.

To be honored by being requested to give the eulogy at the funeral of Dr. Martin Luther King is like asking one to eulogize his deceased son, so close and so precious was he to me.

Our friendship goes back to his student days here at Morehouse. It is not an easy task. Nevertheless I accepted with a sad heart and with full knowledge of my inadequacy to do justice to this good man.

It was my desire that if I predeceased Dr. King he would pay tribute to me on my final day. It was his wish that if he predeceased me I would deliver the homily at his funeral. Fate has decreed that I eulogize him. I wish it might have been otherwise for after all I am three score years and ten and Martin Luther is dead at 39. How strange.

God called the grandson of a slave on his father's side and the grandson of a man born during the Civil War on his mother's side and said to him—Martin Luther—"Speak to America about war and peace. Speak to America about social injustice and racial discrimination. Speak to America about its obligation to the poor and speak to America about nonviolence."

Let it be thoroughly understood that our deceased brother did not embrace nonviolence out of fear or cowardice. Moral courage was one of his noblest virtues. As Mahatma Gandhi challenged the British empire without a sword and won, Martin Luther King, Jr. challenged the interracial injustice of his country without a gun. He had faith to believe that he would win the battle for social justice.

I make bold to assert that it took more courage for Martin Luther to practice nonviolence than it took his assassin to fire the fatal shot. The assassin is a coward. He committed his dastardly deed and fled. When Martin Luther disobeyed an unjust law, he suffered the consequences of his action. He never ran away and he never begged for mercy.

He returned to Birmingham jail to serve his time. Perhaps he was more courageous than soldiers who fight and die on the battlefield.

There is an element of compulsion in their dying. But when Martin Luther faced death again and again and finally embraced it, there was no external pressure. He was acting on an inner urge that drove him on, more courageous than those who advocate violence as a way out, for they carry weapons of destruction for defense. But Martin Luther faced the dogs, the police, the jails, heavy criticism, and finally death, and he never carried a gun, not even a pocket knife to defend himself.

He had only his faith in a just God to rely on and his belief that thrice is he armed who has his quarrels just—the faith that Browning writes about when he says: "One who never turned his back but marched to press forward never doubted that clouds would break, never dreamed that right, though worsted, wrong would triumph...."

Coupled with moral courage was Martin Luther, Jr.'s capacity to love people. Though deeply committed to a program of freedom for Negroes, he had a love and a deep concern for all kinds of people. He drew no distinction between the high and the low, none between the rich and the poor. He believed especially that he was sent to champion the cause of the man farthest down. He would probably have said, "If death had to come I am sure there was no greater cause to die for than fighting to get a just wage for garbage collectors."

This man was suprarace, supranation, supradenomination, supraclass and supraculture. He belonged to the world and to mankind. Now he belongs to posterity.

But there is a dichotomy in all of this. This man was loved by some and hated by others. If any man knew the meaning of suffering, Martin Luther knew—house bombed, living...day-by-day for 13 years under constant threat of death, maliciously accused of being a Communist, falsely accused of being insecure, insincere and seeking the lime-light for his own glory, stabbed by a member of his own race, slugged in a hotel lobby, jailed 30 times, occasionally deeply hurt because his friends betrayed him.

And yet this man had no bitterness in his heart, no rancor in his soul, no revenge in his mind, and he went up and down the length and breadth of this world preaching nonviolence and the receptive power of love.

He believed with all of his heart, mind and soul that the way to peace and brotherhood is through nonviolence, love and suffering. He was severely criticized for his opposition to the war in Vietnam. It must be said, however, that one could hardly expect a prophet of King's commitment to advocate nonviolence at home and violence in Vietnam.

Nonviolence to King was total commitment not only in solving the problems of race in the United States but in solving the problems of the world.

Surely, surely this man was called of God to his work. If Amos and Micah were prophets in the eighth century BC, Martin Luther King, Jr. was a prophet in the 20th century. If Isaiah was called of God to prophecy in his day, Martin Luther was called of God to prophecy in his day. If Hosea was sent to preach love and forgiveness centuries ago, Martin Luther was sent to expound the doctrine of nonviolence and forgiveness in the third quarter of the 20th century.

If Jesus was called to preach the Gospel to the poor, Martin Luther was called to bring dignity to the common man. If a prophet is one who interprets in clear and intelligible language the will of God, Martin Luther Jr. fits that designation. If a prophet is one who does not seek popular causes to espouse, but rather the causes which he thinks are right, Martin Luther qualifies on that score.

No, he was not ahead of his time. No man is ahead of his time. Every man is within his time. Each man must respond to the call of God in his lifetime and not somebody else's time. Jesus had to respond to the call of God in the first century AD and not in the 20th century. He had but one life to give. Jesus couldn't wait. How long do you think Jesus would have had to wait for the constituted authorities to accept him—25 years, 100 years, 1,000 years, never? He died at 33. He couldn't wait. Paul, Copernicus, Martin Luther, the Protestant reformer, Gandhi, and Nehru couldn't wait for another time. They had to act in their lifetimes. No man is ahead of his time.

Abraham staying with his country in obedience to God's call. Moses leading a rebellious people to the Promised Land. Jesus dying on a cross. Gallileo on his knees recanting at 70, Lincoln dying of an assassin's bullet, Woodrow Wilson crusading for a League of Nations, Martin Luther King, Jr. fighting for justice for garbage collectors, none of these men were ahead of their time. With them the time is always right to do that which is right and that which needs to be done.

Too bad, you say, Martin Luther, Jr. died so young. I feel that way, too. But as I have said many times before, it isn't how long one lives but how well. Jesus died at 33, Joan of Arc at 19, Byron and Burns at 36, Keats and Marlowe at 29, and Shelley at 30, Dunbar before 35, John Fitzgerald Kennedy at 46, William Rainey Harper at 49 and Martin Luther King Jr. at 39.

It isn't how long, but how well.

We all pray that the assassin will be apprehended and brought to justice, but make no mistake, the American people are in part responsible for Martin Luther King's death. The assassin heard enough condemnation of King and Negroes to feel that he had public support. He knew that there were millions of people in the United States who wished that King was dead. He had support. The Memphis officials must bear some of the guilt for Martin Luther King's assassination.

The strike should have been settled several weeks ago. The lowest paid man in our society should not have to strike to get a decent wage a century after emancipation and after the enactment of the 13th, 14th, and 15th Amendments. It should not have been necessary for Martin Luther King Jr. to stage marches in Montgomery, Birmingham, Selma and go to jail 30 times trying to achieve for his people those rights which people of lighter hue get by virtue of the fact that they are born white.

We, too, are guilty of murder. It is a time for the American people to repent and make democracy equally applicable to all Americans.

What can we do? We and not the assassin, we and not the President, we and not the apostles of hate, we represent here today America at its best. We have the power to make democracy function so that Martin Luther King and his kind will not have to march.

What can we do? If we love Martin Luther King and respect him as this crowd surely testifies, let us see to it that he did not die in vain. Let us see to it that we do not dishonor his name by trying to solve our problems through rioting in the streets.

Violence was foreign to his nature. He warned that continued riots could produce a Fascist state. But let us see to it also that the conditions that cause riots are promptly removed as the President of the United States is trying to get us to do. Let black and white alike search their hearts and if there be any prejudice in our hearts against interracial or ethnic groups let us exterminate it and let us pray, as Martin Luther would pray if he could: "Father forgive them, for they know not what they do."

If we do this, Martin Luther King Jr. will have died a redemptive death for which all mankind will benefit. Morehouse will never be the same because Martin Luther came by here and the nation and the world will be indebted to him for a century to come.

It is natural, therefore, that we here at Morehouse and Dr. Foster would want to memorialize him to serve as an inspiration to all students who study in this center.

I close by saying to you what Martin Luther King Jr. believed: "If physical death was the price he had to pay to rid America of prejudice and injustice, nothing could be more redemptive." And to paraphrase words of the immortal John Fitzgerald Kennedy, permit me to say that Martin Luther King Jr.'s unfinished work on earth must truly be our own.

EULOGY FOR JACQUELINE KENNEDY ONASSIS
by Senator Edward M. Kennedy
May 23, 1994

Last summer, when we were on the upper deck on the boat at the Vineyard, waiting for President and Mrs. Clinton to arrive, Jackie turned to me and said: "Teddy, you go down and greet the President."

"But," I said, "Maurice is already there."

And Jackie answered: "Teddy, you do it. Maurice isn't running for re-election."

She was always there—for all our family—in her special way.

She was a blessing to us and to the nation—and a lesson to the world on how to do things right, how to be a mother, how to appreciate history, how to be courageous.

No one else looked like her, spoke like her, wrote like her, or was so original in the way she did things. No one we knew ever had a better sense of self.

Eight months before she married Jack, they went together to President Eisenhower's Inaugural Ball. Jackie said later that that's where they decided they liked Inaugurations.

No one ever gave more meaning to the title of First Lady. The nation's capital city looks as it does because of her. She saved Lafayette Square and Pennsylvania Avenue.

Jackie brought the greatest artists to the white House, and brought the Arts to the center of national attention. Today, in large part because of her inspiration and vision, the arts are an abiding part of national policy.

President Kennedy took such delight in her brilliance and her spirit. At a white House dinner, he once leaned over and told the wife of the French Ambassador, "Jackie speaks fluent French. But I only understand one out of every five words she says—and that word is DeGaulle."

And then, during those four endless days in 1963, she held us together as a family and a country. In large part because of her, we could grieve and then go on. She lifted us up, and in the doubt and darkness, she gave her fellow citizens back their pride as Americans. She was then 34 years old.

Afterward, as the eternal fame she lit flickered in the autumn of Arlington Cemetery, Jackie went on to do what she most wanted—to raise Caroline and John, and warm her family's life and that of all the Kennedys.

Robert Kennedy sustained her, and she helped make it possible for Bobby to continue. She kept Jack's memory alive, as he carried Jack's mission on.

Her two children turned out to be extraordinary, honest, unspoiled, and with a character equal to hers. And she did it in the most trying of circumstances. They are her two miracles.

Her love for Caroline and John was deep and unqualified. She reveled in their accomplishments, she hurt with their sorrows, and she felt sheer joy and delight in spending time with them. At the mere mention of one of their names, Jackie's eyes would shine brighter and her smile would grow bigger.

She once said that if you "bungle raising your children nothing else much matters in life." She didn't bungle. Once again, she showed how to do the most important thing of all, and do it right. When she went to work, Jackie became a respected professional in the world of publishing. And because of her, remarkable books came to life. She searched out new authors and ideas. She was interested in everything.

Her love of history became a devotion to historic preservation. You knew, when Jackie joined the cause to save a building in Manhattan, the bulldozers might as well turn around and go home.

She had a wonderful sense of humor—a way of focusing on someone with total attention—and a little girl delight in who they were and what they were saying. It was a gift of herself that she gave to others. And in spite of all her heartache and loss, she never faltered.

I often think of what she said about Jack in December after he died: "They made him a legend, when he would have preferred to be a man." Jackie would have preferred to be just herself, but the world insisted that she be a legend, too.

She never wanted public notice, in part I think, because it brought back painful memories of an unbearable sorrow, endured in the glare of a million lights.

In all the years since then, her genuineness and depth of character continued to shine through the privacy, and reach people everywhere. Jackie was too young to be a widow in 1963, and too young to die now.

Her grandchildren were bringing new joy to her life, a joy that illuminated her face whenever you saw them together. Whether it was taking Rose and Tatiana for an ice cream cone, or taking a walk in Central Park with little Jack as she did last Sunday, she relished being Grand Jackie and showering her grandchildren with love.

Her grandchildren were bringing new joy to her life, a joy that illuminated her face whenever you saw them together. Whether it was taking Rose and Tatiana for an ice cream cone, or taking a walk in Central Park with little Jack as she did last Sunday, she relished being Grand Jackie and showering her grandchildren with love.

At the end, she worried more about us than herself. She let her family and friends know she was thinking of them. How cherished were those wonderful notes in her distinctive hand on her powder blue stationery!

In truth, she did everything she could—and more—for each of us. She made a rare and noble contribution to the American spirit. But for us, most of all she was a magnificent wife, mother, grandmother, sister, aunt, and friend.

She graced our history. And for those of us who knew and loved her—she graced our lives.

EULOGY FOR YITZHAK RABIN
Former Prime Minister of Israel by
his grand-daughter, Noa Ben-Artzi Filosof
November 6, 1995

You will forgive me, for I do not want to talk about peace. I want to talk about my grandfather. One always wakes up from a nightmare. But since yesterday, I have only awakened to a nightmare—the nightmare of life without you, and this I cannot bear. The television does not stop showing your picture; you are so alive and tangible that I can almost touch you, but it is only "almost" because already I cannot.

Grandfather, you were the pillar of fire before the camp and now we are left as only the camp, alone, in the dark, and it is so cold and sad for us. I know we are talking in terms of a national tragedy, but how can you try to comfort an entire people or include it in your personal pain, when grandmother does not stop crying, and we are mute, feeling the enormous void that is left only by your absence.

Few truly knew you. They can still talk a lot about you, but I feel that they know nothing about the depth of the pain, the disaster and, yes, this holocaust, for—at least for us, the family and the friends, who are left only as the camp, without you—our pillar of fire.

Grandfather, you were, and still are, our hero. I want you to know that in all I have ever done, I have always seen you before my eyes. Your esteem and love accompanied us in every step and on every path, and we lived in the light of your values. You never abandoned us, and now they have abandoned you—you, my eternal hero—cold and lonely, and I can do nothing to save you, you who are so wonderful.

People greater than I have already eulogized you, but none of them was fortunate like myself to feel the caress of your warm, soft hands and the warm embrace that was just for us, or your half-smiles which will always say so much, the same smile that is no more, and froze with you. I have no feelings of revenge because my pain and loss are so big, too big. The ground has slipped away from under our feet, and we are trying, somehow, to sit in this empty space that has been left behind, in the meantime, without any particular success. I am incapable of finishing, but it appears that a strange hand, a miserable person, has already finished for me. Having no choice, I part from you, a hero, and ask that you rest in peace, that you think about us and miss us, because we here—down below—love you so much. To the angels of heaven that are accompanying you now, I ask that they watch over you, that they guard you well, because you deserve such a guard. We will love you grandfather, always.

EULOGY FOR YITZHAK RABIN
by Shimon Sheves
November 6,1995

Our Dear Yitzhak, it is almost impossible to speak of you in the past tense. I cannot accept that all of us—family, friends, and all of your admirers—are standing here beside your casket. I cannot accept the fact that an abominable, murderous hand, a hand full of poison and hate, put an end to your life's work, and cut short your energy, your strength, your faith. You were an exemplary warrior and military man, you were a statesman, and a leader from the shoulders up. You were the embodiment of the prickly "Sabra" fruit—rough outside, yet soft, sensitive, and wonderful inside. You were a man in whom the vision and values, wisdom and understanding and the incredible ability to formulate them into action, came together in a rare and wonderful manner. With the spirit of determination, and an extraordinary talent, with great faith, you and only you were justified in the path that stood before your eyes.

You were a wonderfully loved and adored husband, father, and grandfather. I was with you when you worried so much, if all that you hoped for so much, would pass in peace. We all knew, and felt the great love, the rare connection that you had with Leah, Dalia, Yuval, Noaleh, Yonatan, Mikey, Rachel and everyone. If only you know of the love, the admiration, and the nostalgia that they are expressing towards you. They are a wonderful family, and all of us— the close friends and the relatives who admired you— thought of you as the greatest of them all, a strong lion who walked at the head of the camp, flying the flag, and with us following behind you. For me, you were a friend, guide, leader, and great father. We began to work together almost 13 years ago, and since then, our paths have not parted. I had the honor of being by your side in the difficult and great moments.

I followed you with closed eyes, and now I refuse to open them, refuse to believe. I was with you in moments of darkness and mourning, at the death of soldiers and sons; as well as during times of great light and happiness in which we took part in the happiness of people, in developing the country and changing the face of the country and realizing the vision of peace. During all these times, you remained yourself, a man worth becoming associated with, not a man of etiquette, a forthright and determined man, feeling, real, and wise. Oh, how so wise. And because of all of this, I loved you. More than that, I believed in you without reservation. I always knew that if there was a person in whose hands it was possible to put our fate, our future, our well-being and that of our children, it was only you, only Yitzhak Rabin.

You were not dissuaded by intimidation, you were not taken aback by threats. You believed in the People of Israel, in Israelis, and in Israeliness. You believed that a majority of the nation wanted peace and supported the peace process and you. This day, for us, is a difficult day. A day that is difficult not to call by its name—a day of shock, a day of calamity, a day of feeling like an orphan, with a heavy burden, and terribly emptiness.

I have lost a leader and a friend. I said that I have lost a country. I mean that Israel, after this abhorrent murder, will not be the same Israel as it was, in any way, like it was during the life of Yitzhak.

We have lost a very dear man. At this moment, the only thing that is left to us is to remember the nice moments of your life. You fell on a night filled with optimism. You fell on a night full of joy and solidarity. You fell on a night in which you brought the support of the nation for your path, the road of peace, to a peak. Security and peace, peace and security were the values most important to you. All of us must take to our hearts and to our minds what became your legacy on that awful night, and rush not towards violence but, towards peace! With this legacy, we will continue your path; the path that you paved for all of us. You are no longer, but your spirit, your faith, your devotion, the devotion to the path, remain with us.

Yitzhak, I leave you with a salute and a hug. I loved you so very much, a man, a great father, a friend and teacher like you—I will no longer have. In the words of the poet, where are there any more men like this one. There will be peace, Mr. Prime Minister. Farewell, Mr. Prime Minister. Farewell, Yitzhak of us all.

EULOGY FOR YITZHAK RABIN
By Eitan Habers,
Dir. Of Prime Minister's Bureau
November 6, 1995

Yitzhak, this is the final speech. There will be no others. For a generation, for more than 35 years, you have been my guide, my leader, and like a second father to me. Five minutes before the man who shot drew his gun, you sang "The Song of Peace" from a lyric sheet which was handed to you in order, like you always said, not to mumble the words. Yitzhak, you know you had a thousand good qualities, a thousand advantages, you were great, yet singing was not your strong point. You faked the words just a little bit during the song and afterwards, folded the page into four equal parts, as always, and put it into your jacket pocket.

In the hospital, after the doctors and nurses had cried, they handed me the paper which they found in your jacket pocket. Again, the page was folded into four equal parts, as always. Now, I want to read some of the words from the paper, but it is difficult for me. Your blood, your blood Yitzhak, covers the printed words. Your blood on the page of "The Song of Peace." This is the blood which ran out of your body in the final moments of your life and onto the paper between the lines and the words. From this red page, from the blood which screams out to you, I would now like to read these words, which seem like they were written only yesterday. After you sang there, and after you and peace were shot. This is the page:

55

"Let the sun rise
And give the morning light,
The purest prayer
Will not bring us back
He whose candle was snuffed out
And was buried in the dust
A bitter cry won't wake him
Won't bring him back

Nobody will return us
From the dead dark pit
Here—neither the victory cheer
Nor songs of praise will help
So—sing only a song for peace
Do not whisper a prayer
Better sing a song for peace
With a big shout."

Yitzhak, we already miss you.

EULOGY FOR DIANA FRANCES SPENCER
Princess of Wales
by her brother, Charles, the ninth Earl Spencer
September 7, 1997

I stand before you today the representative of a family in grief, in a country in mourning, before a world in shock. We are all united not only in our desire to pay our respects to Diana, but rather in our need to do so.

For such was her extraordinary appeal that the tens of millions of people taking part in this service all over the world via television and radio who never actually met her, feel that they, too, lost someone close to them in the early hours of Sunday morning. It is a more remarkable tribute to Diana than I can ever hope to offer her today.

Diana was the very essence of compassion, of duty, of style, of beauty. All over the world she was a symbol of selfless humanity, a standard-bearer for the rights of the truly down-trodden, a truly British girl who transcended nationality, someone with a natural nobility who was classless, who proved in the last year that she needed no royal title to continue to generate her particular brand of magic.

Today is our chance to say ``thank you'' for the way you brightened our lives, even though God granted you but half a life. We will all feel cheated that you were taken from us so young and yet we must learn to be grateful that you came along at all.

Only now that you are gone do we truly appreciate what we are now without and we want you to know that life without you is very, very difficult.

We have all despaired at our loss over the past week and only the strength of the message you gave us through your years of giving has afforded us the strength to move forward.

There is a temptation to rush to canonize your memory. There is no need to do so. You stand tall enough as a human being of unique qualities not to need to be seen as a saint. Indeed to sanctify your memory would be to miss out on the very core of your being, your wonderfully mischievous sense of humor with the laugh that bent you double, your joy for life transmitted wherever you took your smile, and the sparkle in those unforgettable eyes, your boundless energy which you could barely contain.

But your greatest gift was your intuition, and it was a gift you used wisely. This is what underpinned all your wonderful attributes. And if we look to analyze what it was about you that had such a wide appeal, we find it in your instinctive feel for what was really important in all our lives.

Without your God-given sensitivity, we would be immersed in greater ignorance at the anguish of AIDS and HIV sufferers, the plight of the homeless, the isolation of lepers, the random destruction of land mines. Diana explained to me once that it was her innermost feelings of suffering that made it possible for her to connect with her constituency of the rejected.

And here we come to another truth about her. For all the status, the glamour, the applause, Diana remained throughout a very insecure person at heart, almost child-like in her desire to do good for others so she could release herself from deep feelings of unworthiness of which her eating disorders were merely a symptom.

The world sensed this part of her character and cherished her for her vulnerability, whilst admiring her for her honesty. The last time I saw Diana was on July the first, her birthday, in London, when typically she was not taking time to celebrate her special day with friends but was guest of honor at a charity fund-raising evening.

She sparkled of course, but I would rather cherish the days I spent with her in March when she came to visit me and my children in our home in South Africa. I am proud of the fact that apart from when she was on public display meeting President Mandela, we managed to contrive to stop the ever-present paparazzi from getting a single picture of her.

That meant a lot to her.

These are days I will always treasure. It was as if we'd been transported back to our childhood, when we spent such an enormous amount of time together, the two youngest in the family.

Fundamentally she hadn't changed at all from the big sister who mothered me as a baby, fought with me at school, and endured those long train journeys between our parents' homes with me at weekends. It is a tribute to her level-headedness and strength that despite the most bizarre life imaginable after her childhood, she remained intact, true to herself.

There is no doubt that she was looking for a new direction in her life at this time. She talked endlessly of getting away from England, mainly because of the treatment she received at the hands of the newspapers.

I don't think she ever understood why her genuinely good intentions were sneered at by the media, why there appeared to be a permanent quest on their behalf to bring her down. It is baffling. My own, and only, explanation is that genuine goodness is threatening to those at the opposite end of the moral spectrum.

It is a point to remember that of all the ironies about Diana, perhaps the greatest is this; that a girl given the name of the ancient goddess of hunting was, in the end, the most hunted person of the modern age.

She would want us today to pledge ourselves to protecting her beloved boys William and Harry from a similar fate. And I do this here, Diana, on your behalf. We will not allow them to suffer the anguish that used regularly to drive you to tearful despair.

Beyond that, on behalf of your mother and sisters, I pledge that we, your blood family, will do all we can to continue the imaginative and loving way in which you were steering these two exceptional young men, so that their souls are not simply immersed by duty and tradition but can sing openly as you planned.

We fully respect the heritage into which they have both been born, and will always respect and encourage them in their royal role. But we, like you, recognize the need for them to experience as many different aspects of life as possible, to arm them spiritually and emotionally for the years ahead. I know you would have expected nothing less from us.

William and Harry, we all care desperately for you today. We are all chewed up with sadness at the loss of a woman who wasn't even our mother. How great your suffering is we cannot even imagine.

I would like to end by thanking God for the small mercies he has shown us at this dreadful time; for taking Diana at her most beautiful and radiant and when she had so much joy in her private life.

Above all, we give thanks for the life of a woman I am so proud to be able to call my sister: the unique, the complex, the extraordinary and irreplaceable Diana, whose beauty, both internal and external, will never be extinguished from our minds.

The next three eulogies will be presented with their cluster outlines. It will be valuable for you to see how a good outline creates a road map for writing.

EULOGY FOR ALLAN SCHAEFFER
by his grandson, Garry Schaeffer
February 13, 1993

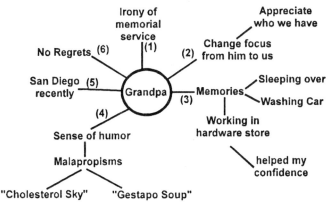

I can't help being struck by an irony. Grandpa was a modest person, one who disliked being the center of attention. As such, I think he would have felt self-conscious about this service, this eulogy, and everyone's attention being centered on him.

Instead, he would have wanted us to change our focus from him to us. He would have wanted us to dwell not on who we have lost, but who we still have. He would have wanted us to use this time to look within and gain a new appreciation of everyone in our lives and find new ways to make our time together more precious. If you will, take a moment with me to do just that.

In this time of transition, from "being with" to "memories of," there is some consolation for me in the good feelings that my memories give me. Memories of staying overnight at my grandparent's house when I was five years old and sleeping between my grandmother and grandfather in their bed. And I remember laughing in the morning when my grandfather would say, "Garry, I woke up in the middle of the night and your foot was in my mouth!" He used to carry on about all the abuse he had endured during the night. I realized years later that he wasn't kidding—I was a restless sleeper.

I have fond memories of living in Glen Head, New York, and being allowed to wash my grandparent's car every Sunday during the summers. And I was thrilled to be paid a whole dollar for it. Of course, if my Grandmother wanted me to, I'd still wash her car for her...for a dollar.

I have fond memories of working alongside my grandfather in the hardware store. From the time I was old enough to open a paper bag, I was working with him at the checkout counter. He would ring up someone's merchandise and then show me which size bag to put it in. He must have been so proud. He'd say to the customers, "I want you to meet my little grandson." I would say hello, put their things in a bag, and say goodbye. I suppose the experience helped form my social skills. To this day I have no problem meeting strangers. I just say hello, put their things in a bag, and say goodbye.

I have many fond memories of my grandfather playing my straight man and being my comedic sparring partner during family dinners. In fact, my grandfather was the King of Malapropisms, and he knew it, but as with anyone with a good sense of humor, he didn't mind laughing at himself or being the butt of a joke. I'll never forget the time we were sitting around the dinner table talking about doctor bills. My father said, "Getting your doctor bill after surgery is enough to make you see stars." My grandfather had to top that; he said, "After my heart surgery, when I saw my doctor bill, I saw a whole cholesterol sky!" That instantly became a family classic.

Another time we were at a big family dinner. The waitress was taking our orders one course at a time. I said, "I'll have the Gespacho soup." My mother said, "I'll also have the Cold Gespacho." My grandfather said, "I'll have the Gestapo Soup."

Most important, for me, however, is the fond memories of—and a great deal of gratitude for having just spent some good quality time with my grandfather—and grandmother—in San Diego less than a month ago. I'm grateful for one particular bit of conversation my grandfather and I had while walking down a street in Tijuana. It was one of those rare moments when he told me about something in his life that hurt him—and I told him that it hurt me, too—and tears came to my eyes because we were sharing our vulnerabilities; it was the stuff of which closeness and love are made.

As we make the transition from "being with" to "memories of," I am consoled in knowing that I have no regrets, no "I wish I had said this or done that." I feel fortunate to have wonderful memories of a fun, generous, caring, supportive, and loving grandfather; one who has enriched my life immeasurably.

EULOGY FOR RON HEIMER
by Garry Schaeffer
March 17, 1994

The following eulogy was delivered by the author at an informal gathering at a private residence about a week after his friend died of AIDS.

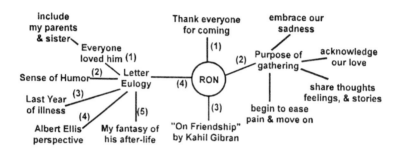

First, I want to thank everyone for coming. Not only for Ron, but for each other. I think it makes us feel better to see how much Ron was loved and how many people cared enough to be here. I know at least four or five people who wanted to be here but couldn't make it. His sister Jan is one of them. I spoke to her yesterday and she asked me to send her love to everyone.

We are gathered to celebrate the life of Ron Heimer and the contributions that he made to all of our lives. We are here to embrace our sadness, acknowledge our love for him, and share some thoughts, feelings, stories, and tributes about someone who affected many of us in profound and enduring ways. In doing so, I am confident that we can begin to ease the pain and move on to a brighter outlook.

dwell not on the grief of your parting, but on the gift that was your love and friendship. For over half my life you occupied the throne that I called, "My Best Friend." You were like a brother to me. You enriched my life immeasurably with your laughter, your jokes, your smiles, your insights, your presence, your joys, your pain, and your frustrations.

The last year has been difficult and I'm sorry if you were embarrassed by it. I will keep the bad times in perspective. They were but a short chapter in the long and wonderful book that was our friendship. That book will always be with me. I will share it with others and amuse them with anecdotes, as I have always done. I will read from that book late at night and first thing in the morning. It will distract me from my work and amuse me when I'm bored. It will be my constant companion and I will never put it on the shelf to gather dust. It is a masterpiece that only we could have created.

Ron, everyone loved you. That was one of the amazing things about you. You were incredibly lovable. My parents loved you as a second son—and I know you loved them. My sister loved you. My grandparents loved you. You were, in virtually every way, a member of our family.

There is no doubt that the way to my heart is through my funny bone, and you were a master at making me laugh. Humor has always been one of our greatest bonds. Our other bonds were my other passions: waterskiing, snow skiing, scuba diving, jazz, cars, and food. But, of course there was more than that and there is no way to break down and analyze the chemistry that makes up a lifetime friendship. Yes, lifetime. You are irreplaceable. You will always be my best friend and my only brother.

Ron, a long time ago you and I went to see Albert Ellis give a lecture on the influence of thoughts on our emotions.

I'm going to practice what he preached. I will try to focus now, not on my sadness of your loss, but on the immense joy that you brought to me as a friend. Every time I become sad because I miss you, I will replace the thought, "I wish you were here" with "I'm so glad you were here." It may be easier said than done, but that is my challenge.

I don't know about an after-life and heaven, but, if there is a heaven I know what it would be for you. Your days would be filled with snow skiing or snow boarding in perfect conditions. Some days you would waterski, other days you would sky dive or scuba dive, some days you would do karate or just watch TV. And your evenings would be spent in a jazz nightclub listening to a band of saints—Buddy Rich, John Coltrane, Billy Holiday, Eddie Jefferson—all the late greats. Be sure to save a seat for me. Unless, of course, someone interesting comes along. And, if I know you, someone will.

EULOGY FOR BARBARA SCHAEFFER
by her grandson, Garry Schaeffer
November 25, 1994

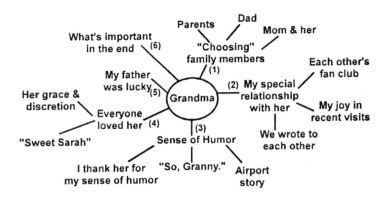

Someone once said, "You can choose your friends, you can choose your spouse, but you can't choose your family." The family you are born into is the outcome of some kind of cosmic roll of the dice. And let's face it, the odds aren't that great.

So it is truly a gift to be born into a wonderful family; and you are especially blessed when you have wonderful parents. I have been blessed with the gift of wonderful parents—a sentiment that I realize and appreciate more as I get older.

My father was blessed with a wonderful mother. She was a loving, devoted, self-less mother. A friend. And a life-long source of joy and comfort.

My father wasn't the only lucky one. To my mother, my grandmother was more than a mother-in-law. Mother-in-law only defines the relationship, it does not describe it. My grandmother was the loving mother that my mother never had; and my mother was the daughter that my grandmother never had. A match made in heaven? No doubt. Clearly, they were each other's gift from above.

My grandmother and I had a special bond. She was my favorite grandmother; and I was her favorite grandson. She was never difficult, cranky, or demanding. She was loving, supportive, and easy to be with. Our relationship was important to both of us. My grandmother wrote to me regularly for many years; and I always found the time to write back.

In the last six months or so when her health was failing her, she got so much joy from my visits. The chemistry between us was incredible—we were each other's fan club.

One of my most fond memories is of my grandmother giving money to me surreptitiously. In a restaurant she would pass a handkerchief full of coins to me under the table. I would accept it and try to keep a straight face because I knew she didn't want my grandfather to know.

It was so cute the way she did that. As I got older, it became increasingly awkward to accept the money, but I realized her giving was a loving gesture, not something to take at face value.

One of the most remarkable things about her was her ability—even when she was ill—to maintain her sense of humor. One time we were walking slowly down the hallway and I said to her, "So...Granny." I never called her granny, but she said, "Granny, you got that right." She loved levity and was always willing to go with the flow. She was always tuned in to appreciating a joke, and usually contributing her own to the banter. At the end of one of my visits here, I went to her apartment before heading to the airport. I was surprised to see her dressed and intending to go to the airport with us. I said, "I'm glad you're coming to the airport; every minute counts." She said, "Ha, you're telling me!"

I have her to thank for my greatest joy in life—my sense of humor and my ability to make people laugh. She was the original comedienne who instilled that quality in my father, who passed it on to me. Laughter is a celebration of life, and my grandmother taught us to celebrate as much and as often as we can. For that, I thank her.

If I had to choose one word to describe my grandmother, it would be sweet. She was very sweet, very lovable. She was loved by everyone. It was a theme we saw repeatedly.

People in her apartment complex adored her. Nurses in the hospital called her "Sweet Barbara." People who knew her in San Diego—even briefly—thought she was wonderful. She was sweet, charming, and never had a bad word for anyone. And if she did, she had the grace to keep it to herself.

I can't get over how lucky my father was to have had his mother for virtually his entire life. That's an incredible gift. It gives a new perspective to having children at a young age. If I had had this insight when I was in my 20's, I would have had children. I wouldn't have gotten married, but I would have had children. My father and mother were very lucky to have been so close to such a special person for so very long.

In the final analysis—when you're up here and everyone else is out there, and the votes are tallied about your life, it doesn't matter what kind of car you drove or what you did for a living. You are remembered for what is important. Did you have a heart? Did you love people and did people love you? Did you give more than take? Were you thoughtful, kind, easy to be with? Did you have an impact on people's lives? Were you fun? Did you have a sense of humor? And ultimately, will you be missed?

To all of these I can say, YES, a resounding YES, about my grandmother. She will be remembered for the richness of the memories and the depth of the feelings that she gave to others. My grandmother has enriched my life beyond measure, and for that, I will always be grateful. She will always hold a special place in my heart.

POEMS FOR EULOGIES

Here are some poems that may work before, during, or after a eulogy. You can find others in libraries and bookstores. You can also ask friends and relatives if they have favorite poems to recommend. Of course, the best poem would be a favorite of the person for whom you are writing the eulogy.

DYLAN THOMAS
by Witter Bynner
from *A Garland For Dylan Thomas*

How could he do it so quickly,
Be together so wanton and wise?
It makes me feel stupid and sickly
To see the consent of his eyes.

He did not feel cheated of wisdom
By not being given its weight.
He knew that he early had risen
Because he had gone to bed late.

DO NOT STAND AT MY GRAVE AND WEEP

by Mary E. Frye

reprinted with permission from
Food For The Soul
edited by Andrea Gambill
(Bereavement Publishing, 1996)

Do not stand at my grave and weep
I am not there. I do not sleep
I am a thousand winds that blow
I am the diamond glints on snow
I am the sunlight on ripened grain
I am the gentle autumn rain

When you awaken
in the mornings hush,
I am the swift uplifting rush
of quiet birds in circled flight.
I am the soft stars that shine at night.

Do not stand at my grave and cry,
I am not there. I did not die.

CROSSING THE BAR
By Alfred, Lord Tennyson

Sunset and evening star,
And one clear call for me!
And may there be no moaning of the bar,
When I put out to sea,

But such a tide as moving seems asleep,
Too fall for sound and foam,
When that which drew from out the boundless deep
Turns again home

Twilight and evening bell,
And after that the dark!
And may there be no sadness of farewell,
When I embark;

For tho' from out our bourne of Time and Place
The flood may bear me far,
I hope to see my Pilot face to face,
When I have crost the bar.

FUNERAL BLUES
by W.H. Auden
From *Four Cabaret Songs for Miss Hedli Anderson*

Stop all the clocks, cut off the telephone,
Prevent the dog from barking with a juicy bone,
Silence the pianos and with muffled drum
Bring out the coffin, let the mourners come.

Let aeroplanes circle moaning overhead
Scribbling on the sky the message He is Dead.
Put crepe bows round the white necks of the
public doves,
Let the traffic policemen wear black cotton gloves.

He was my North, my South, my East and West,
My working week and my Sunday rest,
My noon, my midnight, my talk, my song;
I thought that love would last forever: I was wrong.

The stars are not wanted now; put out every one,
Pack up the moon and dismantle the sun,
Pour away the ocean and sweep up the woods;
For nothing now can ever come to any good.

IN MEMORIUM A.H.H. (an excerpt)
by Alfred, Lord Tennyson

I sometimes hold it half a sin
   To put in words the grief I feel;
   For words, like Nature, half reveal
And half conceal the Soul within.

But, for the unquiet heart and brain,
   A use in measured language lies;
   The sad mechanic exercise,
Like dull narcotics, numbing pain.

In words, like weeds[1], I'll wrap me o'er,
   Like coarsest clothes against the cold:
   But that large grief which these enfold
Is given in outline and no more.

(1. *i.e.*, widow's weeds, garments worn as
symbols of mourning.)

ALL PATHS LEAD TO YOU
by Blanche Shemaker Wagstaff

All paths lead to you
　Where e'er I stray,
You are the evening star
　At the end of day.

All paths lead to you
　Hill-top or low,
You are the white birch
　In the sun's glow.

All paths lead to you
　Where e'er I roam.
You are the lark-song
　Calling me home!

TO A FRIEND
by Grace Stricker Dawson

You entered my life in a causal way,
    And saw at a glance what I needed;
There were others who passed me or met me each day,
    But never a one of them heeded.
Perhaps you were thinking of other folks more,
    Or chance simply seemed to decree it;
I know there were many such chances before,
    But the others—well, they didn't see it.

You said just the thing that I wished you would say,
    And you made me believe that you meant it;
I held up my head in the old gallant way,
    And resolved you should never repent it.
There are times when encouragement means such a lot,
    And a word is enough to convey it;
There were others who could have, as easy as not
    But, just the same, they didn't say it.

There may have been someone who could have done more
    To help me along, though I doubt it;
What I needed was cheering, and always before
    They had let me plod onward without it.
You helped to refashion the dream of my heart,
    And made me turn eagerly to it;
There were others who might have (I question that part)
    But, after all, they didn't do it!

A MILE WITH ME
by Henry Van Dyke

O who will walk a mile with me
    Along life's merry way?
A comrade blithe and full of glee,
Who dares to laugh out loud and free,
And let his frolic fancy play,
Like a happy child, through the flowers gay
That fill the field and fringe the way
    Where he walks a mile with me.

And who will walk a mile with me
    Along life's weary way?
A friend whose heart has eyes to see
The stars shine out o'er the darkening lea,
And the quiet rest at the end o' the day,—
A friend who knows, and dares to say,
The brave, sweet words that cheer the way
    Where he walks a mile with me.

With such a comrade, such a friend,
I fain would walk till journey's end,
Through summer sunshine, winter rain,
And then?—Farewell, we shall meet again!

The following poem is wonderful, however, to use it in a eulogy, I would change some of it to the past tense. I would tell my audience, "This is a poem entitled, 'Love,' by Roy Croft. I have changed it slightly for this occasion."

To illustrate, I have changed the first stanza to:

I love you,
Not only for what you were,
But for what I was
When I was with you.

LOVE
by Roy Croft

I love you,
Not only for what you are,
But for what I am
When I am with you.

I love you,
Not only for what
You have made of
yourself,
But for what
You are making of me.

I love you
For the part of me
That you bring out;

I love you
For putting your hand
Into my heaped-up heart
And passing over
All the foolish, weak things
That you can't help
Dimly see there,
And for drawing out
Into the light
All the beautiful belongings
That no one else had looked
Quite far enough to find.

(Continued)

79

I love you because you
Are helping me to make
Of the lumber of my life
Not a tavern
But a temple;
Out of the works
Of my every day
Not a reproach
But a song.

I love you
Because you have done
More than any creed
Could have done
To make me good,
And more than any fate
Could have done
To make me happy.

You have done it
Without a touch,
Without a word,
Without a sign.
You have done it
By being yourself.
Perhaps that is what
Being a friend means,
After all.

MISS YOU
by David Cory

Miss you, miss you, miss you;
Everything I do
Echoes with the laughter
And the voice of You.
You're on every corner,
Every turn and twist,
Every old familiar spot
Whispers how you're missed.

Miss you, miss you, miss you!
Everywhere I go
There are poignant memories
Dancing in a row.
Silhouette and shadow
Of your form and face,
Substance and reality
Everywhere displace.

Oh, I miss you, miss you!
God! I miss you, Girl!
There's a strange, sad silence
'Mid the busy whirl,
Just as tho' the ordinary
Daily things I do
Wait with me, expectant
For a word from You.

Miss you, miss you, miss you!
Nothing now seems true
Only that 'twas heaven
Just to be with You.

ON FRIENDSHIP
excerpted and edited from
The Prophet by Kahil Gibran

Your friend is your needs answered.

He is your field which you sow with love and reap
with thanksgiving.

And he is your board and your fireside, for you come
to him with your hunger and you seek him for peace.
When your friend parts from you, grieve not; for that
which you love most in him may be more clear in his
absence, as the mountain is more clear from the plain.

And in the sweetness of memory let there be laughter,
and the sharing of pleasures. For in the dew of little
things the heart finds its morning and is refreshed.

The following eight contributions came from an excellent book
of inspirational poetry and quotations. Forever Remembered by
Dan Zadra, is a compilation of cherished messages of hope,
love, and comfort from courageous people who have lost a
loved one. It can be found in local bookstores or ordered directly
from Compendium, Inc. at 800-914-3327.

I loved my friend
He went away from me
There's nothing more to say
The poem ends soft as it began—
I loved my friend.
— Langston Hughes

THE STORY OF TWO SHIPS
from the Talmud

In a harbor, two ships sailed—one setting forth on a voyage, the other coming home to port. Everyone cheered the ship going out, but the ship sailing in was scarcely noticed. To this, a wise man said, "Do not rejoice over a ship setting out to sea, for you cannot know what storms it may encounter. Rather, rejoice over the ship that has safely reached port and brings its passengers home in peace."

And this is the way of the world: When a child is born, all rejoice; when someone dies, all weep. Why don't we do the opposite, for no one can tell what trials await a newborn child; but when a mortal dies in peace, we should rejoice, for s/he has completed a long journey, and there is no greater boon than to leave this world with the imperishable crown of a good name.

After Gracie Allen died, George Burns found a note in her dresser drawer. It read...

> George,
>> Don't put a period where God
>> intended a comma.
>>> Love,
>>>> Gracie

Because of you, I love a little more.
Because of you, I take time
to give an extra kiss goodbye.
Because of you, I have a new favorite song.
Because of you, there may be dust
on the window sill, but I don't care.

Because of you, I live today,
before I worry about tomorrow.
Because of you, I don't give up quite as fast.
Because of you, I still believe in rainbows.
Because of you, now I can help or listen more.
Because of you, today I am me.

—Eileen Wernsman,
Loving Arms Newsletter

Is this the end? I know it cannot be,
Our ships shall sail upon another sea;
New islands yet shall break upon our sight,
New continents of love and truth and might.

—John White Chadwick

"All the darkness in the world cannot
extinguish the light of a single candle."
—Maria Gaulier

And if I go, while you're still here...
know that I live on,
vibrating to a different measure
behind a thin veil you cannot see through.

You will not see me,
so you must have faith.

I wait for the time when
we can soar together again,
both aware of each other.

Until then, live your life to its fullest
and when you need me,
just whisper my name in your heart,
...I will be there.

　　　　　　　—Emily Dickinson

How do I love thee?
Let me count the ways.
I love thee to the depth and breadth and height
My soul can reach, when feeling out of sight
For the ends of Beings and ideal Grace...
I love thee with the breath,
Smiles, tears, of all my life!—and, if
God choose,
I shall but love thee better after death

　　　　　—Elizabeth Barrett Browning
　　　　　Sonnets from the Portugese

Excerpt From
TURN AGAIN TO LIFE
by Mary Lee Hall

If I should die and leave you here awhile,
Be not like others, sore undone, who keep
Long vigils by the silent dust, and weep.
For my sake - turn again to life and smile,
Nerving thy heart and trembling hand to do
Something to comfort other hearts than thine.
Complete those dear unfinished tasks of mine
And I, perchance, may therein comfort you.

Katrina's Sun Dial
by Henry Van Dyke

Time is too slow for those who wait,
too swift for those who fear,
too long for those who grieve,
too short for those who rejoice,
but for those who love, time is eternity.
Hours fly, flowers die,
new days, new ways pass by,
Love stays.

THE HEALING POWER
OF WRITING

"Give sorrow words."
— William Shakespeare

On some level, everyone knows how therapeutic writing can be. Many of us have written angry letters that were never intended to be mailed—and hopefully were not mailed—and felt better for having written them.

Writing can provide a powerful catharsis. It brings up memories and rekindles feelings. It allows you to revisit emotions that are important to the healing process. For this reason, whether you write a eulogy or not, try to find the time to get your feelings on paper. Express them. It has been said, "The only way out is through." The fastest way through the grieving process is to feel the depth of your loss.

There are many ways to use writing as a tool to help you. Some people keep a journal or diary; others write letters, stories, or poems; some people send e-mail to friends or relatives. It is not important *what* you do, as long as you do *something*.

An unknown author wrote: "To live in the past, to allow ghosts and nightmares to blind you to the pleasures and possibilities of the present, is to dishonor the memory of the dead."

Julia Cameron, in her book, The Artist's Way, gives readers a daily writing assignment . Readers are instructed to write every morning. Cameron calls it, "morning papers." We can call it, "mourning papers." The assignment is to set aside a block of time each morning to write three pages about anything. Write long-hand rather than on a typewriter or computer. Apparently writing long-hand creates a better connection between the hand, brain, and the heart.

Don't worry about the writing process when doing this exercise. Disregard spelling, grammar, and punctuation. Forget about technicalities such as being redundant or writing incomplete thoughts or feelings. The goal is not to write something that is good—or something that will ever be read again—but to write simply for the sake of getting your thoughts and feelings out of your system.

Mourning papers can—and should—include fantasies, goals, complaints, frustrations, memories, regrets, joys, and so on. Nothing is too trivial or monumental. You can complain about someone at work or about a neighbor's barking dog. You can write about your hopes or sorrows. You can create a grocery list. You can create goals. You can create a better life for yourself or you can work on your most immediate needs.

In your writing, have a conversation with your loved one. Work to resolve unfinished business. If appropriate, ask for forgiveness or lovingly give your forgiveness. Express your love for the person repeatedly.

The only rule is there are no rules. Let whatever is on your mind flow onto the paper. Unburden yourself of pain, sorrow, fears, regrets, and so on. Go with the flow of your thoughts. Make it a stream-of-consciousness.

This is a very powerful exercise during which you will discover:

- The process is truly enjoyable, even if you resist getting started.
- Your thoughts will flow quickly, with the important ones pushing up to the surface with great force.
- It is easy to fill up three pages.
- You might want to stop to cry, especially if you are currently in pain. Don't hold back, the writing can wait. Bringing up the pain, although unpleasant, is part of working through it. I'm not a therapist, but I know that repressing feelings is counter-productive. Tears water our growth.
- The process helps you get rid of petty complaints and obsessions.
- You will look forward to these morning writing sessions.

You bought this book to help you write a eulogy, but clearly the importance and impact of writing can go far beyond a eulogy. Use writing as a form of therapy—on a regular basis or just when needed.

THE LIVING EULOGY

It is a shame people are eulogized only after they die. Why not have them enjoy your love and appreciation while they are alive! A little courage, effort, and creativity on your part can be rewarding for everyone involved.

A beautiful example of a living eulogy can be found on the internet site: www.alanbaskin.net. It pays tribute to a remarkable man who has loving friends worldwide.

What can you do? Here are three possibilities:

1) Contact people who know and value your loved one. Ask them to send you letters of tribute that include fond memories, etc. of your loved one. Give contributors a hard deadline, then compile the letters into an album to present to the recipient. If you are web-savvy, create an internet site for this purpose. You can also contact www.funerals-online.com about hosting a living eulogy.

2) Ask a small number of people to write living eulogies. Invite them and your loved one to dinner. After dinner, explain the reason for the gathering and invite everyone to read what they have written for the guest of honor.

3) If you prefer to work alone, write a living eulogy and set up a time to read it to your loved one, with or without dinner.

It takes courage to deliver a living eulogy, but it is a tremendous growth and sharing opportunity. A friend told me about her experience delivering a living eulogy to her mother. Her tribute set the stage for the most heartfelt and deeply significant conversations they had ever shared. They discussed their relationship, their hopes and fears, their disappointments, and other sensitive subjects. They resolved some old, nagging issues and achieved a new closeness for which both were grateful. The experience turned out to be a profound gift.

You can make this happen for you and your loved one, too.

INDEX